# THE ULTIMATE SLOW COOKER RECIPE BOOK

## Easy and Delicious Meals for Every Day incl. BONUS Keto Diet Recipes and Meal Planner

**BETH GARDNER**

# TABLE OF CONTENTS

# How Slow Cookers Work

In this chapter we are going to not only look at what a slow cooker is but also how they work. Slow cooker were immensely popular in the 70s and has been a must have cooking appliance for more than 40 years. The idea of slow cooking is simple, and as the name suggests all you do is put your food into a container and let it cook slowly.

Imagine this scenario, it is winter, freezing cold, you have had a particularly difficult day at work. The very thought of having to cook a meal when you get home fills you with utter dread, then you remember you are prepared! As you open the door to your house the delightful smell of stew makes your mouth water. Although there has been no-one around you have a nutritious and welcoming dinner and it is all thanks to your slow cooker.

You will be amazed at the things that you can do courtesy of your slow cooker, and it is used on hog roasts and barbeque pits as this allows the food to cook at a low temperature over a prolonged of time which allows the meat to become tender. You can slow cook food using a dry heat, on a roaster or oven fashion or you can use liquid in the cooking process to give you a moist consistency of the food. Moisture can be used in a uniquely as it seals the food during the cooking process and as the food goes through the cooking process it releases steam, the condensation collects in the slow cooker and acts in the same way as a baster.

The first electric slow cooker was available and became a must have in the 1970s kitchen, with the first versions offered in chic colours such as gold and avocado which in turn also matched with the décor in the kitchen. However, the 80s saw the surge of the microwave which became the latest popular gadget everyone wanted for their kitchen and the slow cooker got left on the shelf. However, people have turned back to their humble slow cooker and there are numerous cookery books which are dedicated purely to the tasty recipes that you can prepared with your slow cooker.

Manufacturers have also picked up on this trend by developing more stylish and new versions of this classic device and this has led to the revival over the past decade as a must have piece of cookery equipment for cooks who simply do not have enough hours in their day.

# The Slow Cooker Device: How It Evolved

The slow cooker origins began with an electric bean pot and this device was created in 1960s with a sole use to steep dry beans. The Electric Bean Pot was produced by the manufacturer West Bend. Naxon Utilities Corporation were the first to develop a rival to the electric bean pot which they named the Beanery. This company is still operating today but now goes by the name of Jarden and in 1971 they acquired Naxon and released a upgraded and remodelled version of the Beanery which we have all come to love as the slow cooker which had the capability to produce an entire meal in just the one pot. There is also a study that was undertaken by the brand Betty Crocker Kitchen which showed that at least 80% of American households owns at least one or more slow cooker.

## Slow Cooker Elements

There are three main components that make up a slow cooker, these are the outer shell, the inner food container, and a lid. The outer shell is constructed of metal and contains all the heating coils required for cooking the food, but the coils are built into the outer shell, so they are fully protected. The inner container is referred to as the crock and this is constructed using ceramic that is glazed and this fits snugly within the container. There are slow cookers where you can remove the inside container, ideal for when it comes to cleaning it! The final part of the slow cooker is the lid that is designed to fit perfectly to ensure none of the steam can escape during the cooking process.

The slow cooker cooks by combining the wattage and time. When you turn on your slow cooker the coil heats up and transfers the heat from the outer shell to the space which is between the outer shell and crock, the base wall of the stoneware crock. This type of heat warms the pot to somewhere in between 180 – 300 degrees Fahrenheit (80 – 145 degrees Celsius.) This way of heat transferal cooks the ingredients gently and they simmer gently on a low temperature setting until the food is cooked perfectly.

The process continues as the food cooks because it releases moisture which the lid ensures does not escape. The moisture creates a vacuum from the edge of the crock with the lid, and this transfer the moisture to the food as well as helping the food to cook. The lid is vital to the whole inner cooking process.

Typically, a slow cooker offers three cooking settings which are low, high, and off. There are programmable slow cookers and once the food is cooked, it will switch settings to keep the food within at the correct temperature, without it burning or drying out.

## Slow Cooker Benefits

You can prepare healthy and nutritious meals in no time using a slow cooker. We all live hectic lives whether it is the pressures of work, have children to look after or you simply want to free up some extra me time. Your answer is to use a slow cooker, as meals can be assembled in the morning, placed in your slow cooker and when you arrive home your dinner is ready and waiting, better still there is no mess and not too much washing up either!

## Little Cost with a Slow Cooker

There are little costs associated with slow cooker cooking. After the initial purchase of your slow cooker as the device uses a minimal amount of electricity and you are not losing the heat that you would if you were using a standard oven.

Using a slow cooker for cooking is a smart choice economically as you can use less expensive meat as the condensation created during cooking self-bastes the food and tougher joints will be tender, thanks to the cooking process. Using your slow cooker to cook vegetables allows them to absorb the stocks and other cooking ingredients making them far tastier with a full flavour. The best thing about using a slow cooker is the time and money you can save without having to sacrifice the taste.

The settings on a slow cooker let you choose the length of time and temperature that you want your meal to be cooked at. It is totally safe to cook using the low setting but if you are at home during the first hour the American authorities advise that all food should be cooked on high for one hour before adjusting the temperature to ensure that the food is completely cooked right the way through.

# Variations of Slow Cookers

When slow cookers first hit the market there was one style, however they have evolved immensely over the years and now they are available in a variety of shapes and sizes. You can purchase manual models, models that are programmable, models that come complete with a digital timer device or a top of the range slow cooker/ that has all of the above functions in one cooker. There are even slow cookers that have been designed to heat up dips which can be useful, particularly if you are hosting a party. Slow cooker have been produced as either oval or round so that they can be used to cook most types of food and the size/liquid capacity is 7 quarts which is the equivalent of 6.6 litres.

# What Cooks Best in a Slow Cooker

Meat is one of the most popular things people cook in their slow cooker. It is important that you defrost the meat beforehand as it will take too long to cook. When you cook meat, it must be heated to 140 degrees F / 60 degrees C, this is important as at these temperatures any bacteria are killed. You also need to make sure that your meat has an internal temperature that is within current guidelines. When you decide to cook chicken, this should still have the skin on as this helps the meat to remain moist through the entire cooking process.

If you want to cook vegetables in your slow cooker be mindful that there is more preparation required and they all need to be cut in the same shape, length etc so that they all cook at the same time. I have found that when I want to make an entire meal using my slow cooker I put the vegetables layered at the bottom of the pot and cover with the meat. Another point to be aware of is that there are many dishes that look fine particularly recipes that are heavy on tomato, however you should consider browning the meat prior to cooking particularly if you want to create a visual feast!

If you plan to cook a stew which is based on meat stock, I suggest that you brown the meat thoroughly before adding it to your slow cooker. Slow cookers drain the colour from most meat when it is cooked therefore it is important not only for appearance but also for flavour that the pieces or joints of meat are caramelised. There are slow cookers that can sear the meat in the cooker or have a removable inner pot that can be used on the hob to save you on the washing up!

## Winter Warmers

Studies in Women's Magazines have reported that amongst the favourite slow cooker meals are stews and soups, this is due to the design of slow cookers and the fact that they were made to cook food on the lowest setting allowing it to simmer for a long time. Not only this they take no time at all to prepare, literally all you need do is place your soup ingredients in the pot, add water to cover and if you need additional water just bring the soup to the boil so that the cooking temperature does not drop, add your water and return the soup to simmer.

It may surprise you to know that spreads and dips are another type of foods that cook incredibly well in a slow cooker. The low setting is ideal to keep any cheese-based dips warm without the ingredients burning, and this is always a great way to maintain the spreads and dips to prevent the ingredients congealing.

I was surprised to find out that grains can be cooked perfectly in a slow cooker. Cracked wheat, rice porridge and oatmeal all cook beautifully overnight and when you wake up you have a nutritious breakfast waiting for you. You can also cook bread and bread-based meals such as stuffing as the low heat setting assist the dough for the bread to rise.

Amongst other dishes that I did not know could be cooked in slow cookers were deserts, ok rice pudding might be an obvious choice, but you can also make all manner of hot deserts as well and cakes.

Some recipes call for adding ingredients towards the end of the cooking time, this is because the ingredients cannot tolerate the way a slow cooker cooks. Many spices and herbs can become far more concentrated when used in slow cooking so you may need to try the cooking process a few times and add just what you need at the end of your cooking. There are also a number of dairy products, seafood and vegetables will lose their texture and flavour if they simmer for too long, therefore if your recipes states that these ingredients should be added at the end of the cooking process follow the instruction precisely.

## Safety Notices

Although slow cookers have been designed so that you can cook and heat your food properly or several hours you still need to undertake the safety advise. Although most of the safety advise is obvious, you would be surprised how easily these things get overlooked.

The first thing you should never do is to fill your inner container with more than two thirds of liquid and never remove the lid whilst the food is cooking as the lid maintains the optimum cooking conditions in your slow cooker. Every now and again you should test your slow cooker to make sure it is heating up properly and that it can cook the food to the right temperature.

# How to Test Your Slow Cooker

When you are ready to test that your slow cooker fill it with about two thirds of water, then add the lid and choose to cook for 8 hours on the low setting. Before the water cools monitor the temperature and if this is 180 degrees F or higher your slow cooker is working perfectly and safe for you to use. If the temperature is below 180 degrees F the heating element may not be working properly and therefore should not be used as it may not be able to cook the food well enough and all the way through.

Slow cookers run using a minimal wattage; therefore it is fine and safe to leave it switched on even when you are not at home. The base of the slow cooker does get warm, but this kitchen appliance has been designed to ensure that it does not overheat or set your kitchen on fire.

The base of your slow cooker should never be immersed in water. If you cannot remove the inner pot, you can simply wash out and sponge off any spills or food residue.

When a slow cooker is exposed to extreme temperature the insert can crack and because of this the insert is not suitable for freezing or to be used with any form of direct heat. A hot slow cooker should not be placed on a cold kitchen top, and you should never pour cold water into a hot slow cooker as it will break.

Remember to thaw poultry and meat completely before adding them to your slow cooker, and prior to serving check that they are hot enough.

When a recipe calls for beans it is vital that you remember that dry beans should not be used in a slow cooker. Dry beans particularly kidney beans carry a toxin which can result in severe abdominal pain coupled with vomiting and an upset stomach. By soaking and boiling the beans the toxins can be eliminated however the temperature in a slow cooker never heats to a high enough temperature therefore if you are planning on using dry beans soak them for at least 14 hours then rinse and boil them for 15 minutes. The safest way would be to use canned beans as these will have gone through the stringent steps before they were canned.

# Change Your Favourite Recipes

Most recipes for casseroles can easily be modified to use a slow cooker however the ingredients will not be subjected to the liquid evaporation that takes place when the food is simmered on a hob or in an oven. Generally, you should reduce the liquid by one third if you are going to use your slow cooker to cook a regular recipe.

If you need to thicken a sauce use one tablespoon of cornflour dissolved in a cup if the sauce, this can then be transferred back into the pot and cooked for another 10 – 15 minutes until the sauce is as thick as you like it.

## Getting Your Settings Right

As we have already discussed there are different temperature settings when it comes to slow cookers. The basic cookers have a high and a low setting whilst the more advances models have a low, medium, high and auto settings. These settings are designed to suit different foods and recipes.

- The high setting is the recommended way to cook pale meats such as turkey and chicken, so that the meat can be cooked for 4 – 6 hours and at a higher heat.
- The medium setting is used to cook red meat and is useful when you want to cook things quickly but not losing the slow cooker benefits. These results will not be as good as cooking the meat on low for longer.
- The low setting is best for cooking the cheaper portions of red meat, because the connective tissues in the meat are broken down, cooking this way usually takes at least 9 hours.
- The automatic cooking setting begins cooking on high and after the first hour it switches and carries on cooking on a low heat.

There are slow cookers that have a keep warm or hold function and this is great if your meal is delayed as the food will not dry out and it also stays hot.

# Slow Cookers – Advantages and Disadvantages

Like all kitchen appliances the slow cooker has both advantages and disadvantages, and this is what we are now going to look at.

## Advantages

The top advantage with a slow cooker must be the amount of time you can save. Time is something we all lack due to the hectic lives we live, and a slow cooker can give us that back. In the morning add your ingredients and let them cook all day, when you get home at the end of a hard day you have a delicious healthy meal waiting for you.

More emphasis is placed on healthier eating that ever before and the slow cooker is the perfect partner. Temperatures and high heat work with food in two ways starting with breaking the nutrients in your food down and these then create harmful chemical structures which have been linked to Alzheimer's, renal problems, and diabetes. Using your slow cooker to cook your food on a low heat setting or temperatures prevent the nutrients from breaking down and the food keeps all the nutrients and the harmful chemicals are kept at bay. By slow cooking, your food will also be flavoursome and will not burn, overcook, or lose its flavours.

The final advantage has to be the amount of money you can save as the ingredients used are relatively inexpensive, you can make your meals last for more than one day and because you are only using a single pot you use far less gas or electricity.

## Disadvantages

Unfortunately, most things that have advantages also have disadvantages and your slow cooker is no exception. Condensation is one of the disadvantages of cooking with a slow cooker as the condensation created by the steam on the lid drips into your food and can result in the flavours and spices being diluted which can leave the food tasting bland.

On the flip side if you are using spices such as cinnamon or thyme in your slow cooking and they simmer for a prolonged period of time you can end up with a flavour that is overpowering in this case you should use far less than the recipe advises.

There are some recipes that simply do not work in a slow cooker. Recipes that specify a large piece of meat or ingredients that must be browned before they are cooked are not right for slow cooking.

Overall, if you look at any recipe/cookbook created for slow cooking you can see how versatile this appliance can be and why it is a must have for your kitchen. It is so easy to combine ingredients within minutes, then let it do its thing until you are ready to eat.

# Frequently Asked Questions

When I first starting cooking with a slow cooker there were a lot of questions that I wanted to find answers for, the most popular are shown here to help you to use your slow cooker/ to its full capacity.

## What cheap cuts of meat are suitable for slow cooking?

You can cook most meats in your slow cooker and as the meats are more cost effective you can experiment to find out what you prefer. Meats that I have found cook particularly well are mutton shoulder, ox cheek and beef shin. Generally, the more work the muscle in the meat does the better it will be when it is slow cooked. The shoulder of an animal is usually tough but this benefits from slow cooking as the cooking process softens it. There is a long list of cheaper cuts of meat that will slow cook perfectly including but not limited to pig's knuckles, trotters and cheeks, all cuts of beef, lamb shank and mutton shoulder, ox tail and cheeks.

## Is it possible to roast meat in a slow cooker?

Yes, you can roast meat in your slow cooker and as it uses about 246 watts it is more energy efficient, as your oven will use approximately 700 watts. If you plan to use your slow cooker/ for roasting it would be more beneficial to purchase an oval shaped pot as the joints will fit easier than they would in a round cooker/pot.

## Is a slow cooker suitable for vegetarian cooking?

Peas, lentils, and dried beans can be cooked perfectly in a slow cooker. All you need to remember is that they must be soaked overnight then boiled to dispel any toxins.

## Other creations using a slow cooker

You can use your slow cooker to create a tasty pudding, just put the ingredients into separate bowls, then place these in the inner container. Add boiling water in between the bowls so that half of the pot is submersed in water and then leave the puddings to poach.

Slow cooking is also a great way to make jam and it can reduce the preparation time as it will soften the fruit whilst ensuring that it does not dry out. Just slice your fruit and cook overnight on the low setting and you have a perfect base for your jam.

## Can you really save time using a slow cooker?

If you want to create a quick and easy dinner, two to ten hours sounds like a long time and although you will need to prep the food either the night before or in the morning. However, when you have done all your prep you add the ingredients to the pot, turn it on and there is nothing else to do until you are ready to eat.

## How long will it take to cook my food in a slow cooker?

You need to check the instructions that come with the slow cooker when it comes to cooking times, as the wattage and heat settings do vary dependent on the model of slow cooker you are using. As a rough estimation you can use the timings given for converting oven to stove top recipes.

## Other ways to use a slow cooker

There are some surprising ways you can use your slow cooker; we have already mentioned how good it is for making jams and it is also a brilliant way to create chutney. You can cook your porridge through the night, so you have a piping hot breakfast ready when you wake up the following morning.

You can boil a chicken carcass with some vegetables and water and in no time, you will have created a rich and flavoursome stock. Puddings such as rice pudding, steamed puddings, and all in one pudding taste fabulous too.

## Can you use your slow cooker in the summer?

When it comes to using a slow cooker you do not need to limit your cooking to stews and soups as there is a plethora of recipes that you can make work in your slow cooker making it the perfect kitchen appliance all year round. Foods such as aubergines or peppers can be reduced in a slow cooker/ and make the perfect toppings for pizzas or in warm salads.

## What is meant by the phrase 'dump bag'?

A dump bag is simply a bag of ingredients that you have prepared and frozen. These bags are ready to 'dump' into your slow cooker. The benefits of cooking in this way does allow you to make batches ahead which helps to cut down on prep time.

# Final Thoughts

The slow cooker is a truly versatile kitchen appliance and is considered indispensable by most people that use them. The thing that makes the food taste so great is also the biggest disadvantage of a slow cooker and this is the slow way it cooks. Having said that, provided you plan and prep in advance this appliance really is like having another chef in your kitchen lending a hand.

# Breakfast

# Breakfast Casserole with Cheesy Potatoes

*Time: 3 hours 30 minutes / Serving 10*
*Net Carbs: 10% (31g / 1.09oz) Fiber: 13% (3g / 0.10oz) Fat: 38% (25g / 0.88oz)*
*Protein: 13g / 0.46oz. Kcal: 400*

## Ingredients:

- 450g / 1lb of bacon, cooked and chopped
- 75g / ½ cup of chopped onion
- 450g / 16oz sour cream
- 300g / 10 ¾oz condensed cream of chicken soup
- 130g / 4.6oz chopped green chillies
- ½ teaspoon salt
- ¼ teaspoon black pepper
- 850g / 30oz frozen shredded hash potatoes, thawed
- 230g / 8oz grated Cheddar cheese
- 2 tbsp butter, melted
- Chopped chives if desired

## Instructions:

1. Spray a 5- or 6-quart slow cooker with cooking spray of your choice

2. Mix together the cooked bacon, onion, sour cream, condensed soup, green chillies, salt and pepper in a large mixing bowl. Make sure to mix it well

3. Into the bowl, carefully add the hash browns and cheese; mix well

4. Transfer this mixture to the slow cooker and pour the melted butter over the top

5. Cover the mix with a large kitchen towel and place the slow cooker lid on top of the towel – this will prevent the condensation dripping onto your hash browns and making them soggy

6. Cook on a high heat for 3 to 4 hours and rotate the dish insert every 1 ½ hours

7. Cook the mixture until it is heated thoroughly, and the edges are beginning to go golden brown

8. Garnish with chopped chives and serve

Note: You can substitute the bacon for 1 lb of cooked bulk pork breakfast sausage if you would prefer

# Breakfast Casserole Tex-Mex-Style

*Time: 3 hours 50 minutes / Serving 10*
*Net Carbs: 9% (27g / 0.95oz) Fat: 50% (32g / 1.13oz)*
*Protein: 25g / 0.88oz. Kcal: 500*

## Ingredients:

- 450g / 1lb ground pork

- 30g / 1oz taco seasoning mix

- 80ml / 1/3 cup of water

- 8 eggs

- 240ml / 1 cup half and half

- 130g / 4.5oz chopped green chilies

- 230g / 8oz grated Cheddar Cheese

- 115g / 4oz grated Monterey Jack Cheese

- 850g / 30oz frozen shredded hash brown potatoes, thawed

- 230g / 8oz cream cheese, cut into 1/2-inch cubes

- If desired: chopped tomatoes, sliced or diced green onions, salsa, chopped cilantro and sour cream

## Instructions:

1. Spray a 5- or 6-quart slow cooker with a cooking spray of your choice

2. In a non-stick skillet (10-inches), cook pork for approximately 5-7 minutes on medium-high heat until no longer pink; stir frequently and drain once cooked

3. Stir in the water and taco seasoning mix; cook over medium heat for one minute

4. In a large bowl mix the eggs and half and half with a whisk; stir in the green chillies, hash brown potatoes, shredded cheeses, and seasoned pork, now cooked. Carefully stir in the cubes of cream cheese

5. Transfer the mixture into the slow cooker

6. Cover the mix with a kitchen towel and place the slow cooker lid on top of the towel – this will prevent the condensation dripping onto the casserole during cooking

7. Cook the mixture on a high heat for 3 to 3 ½ hours, rotating the dish insert every 1 ½ hours

8. Cook until the casserole is set, and the central temperature is 74C / 165F

9. Top with the remaining ingredients

Note: To spice things up, add ¼ teaspoon of ground cayenne pepper with the taco seasoning mix and serve with jalapeno chillies

# Monkey Bread

*Time: 3 hours / Serving 10*
*Net Carbs: 59g / 0.27oz (20%) Fat: 20g / 1.96oz (30%)*
*Protein: 7g / 0.37oz Kcal: 440*

## Ingredients:

- 🍽 57g / 1/4 cup melted butter
- 🍽 350g / 12.4oz Pillsbury™ refrigerated cinnamon rolls with icing
- 🍽 6 eggs
- 🍽 120g / ½ cup whipping cream
- 🍽 1 teaspoon ground cinnamon
- 🍽 1 teaspoon vanilla
- 🍽 350g / 1 cup of real maple syrup

## Instructions:

1. Spray a 5-quart slow cooker with a cooking spray of your choice

2. Pour the melted butter into the slow cooker

3. Separate the dough from the Pillsbury cans into 8 rolls and set the icing to one side

4. Cut each of the rolls into 8 pieces and places these in the slow cooker with the butter

5. In a medium bowl, beat the eggs and add the whipping cream, vanilla, and cinnamon; beat this mix until it is blended well

6. Pour this mixture over the roll pieces and drizzle with 175g / ½ cup of the syrup

7. Cover and cook on a low heat for 2 hours and 30 minutes, check to make sure the temperature in the centre of the rolls is approximately 71C / 160F

8. Drizzle the cooked monkey bread with the icing and remaining syrup before serving

Note: Serve this up with your favourite seasonal fruits such as strawberries, raspberries, and blackberries for a fruity breakfast

# Hot Chocolate Oatmeal

*Time: 6 hours and 20 minutes / Serving 6*
*Net Carbs: 27g / 0.95oz (9%) Fat: 1 ½g / 0.05oz (2%)*
*Protein: 2g / 0.07oz Kcal: 130*

## Ingredients:

- 1,200ml / 5 cups of water
- 160g / 1 cup steel-cut oats
- 70g / 1/3 cup brown sugar
- 70g / 1/3 cup instant hot chocolate mix
- ½ teaspoon salt
- If desired: Chocolate chips and additional brown sugar to serve

## Instructions:

1. Spray a 4- or 5-quart slow cooker with a cooking spray of your choice
2. Mix together in a large mixing bowl the water and oats; transfer this mix into the slow cooker
3. Cover and cook on a low setting for 6 hours, or until the oats are cooked through thoroughly and all of the liquid has been absorbed
4. Stir in brown sugar, hot chocolate mix and salt before serving
5. Serve with chocolate chips and extra brown sugar if needed

Note: Add one of your five-a-day by adding slices of banana to the top! Cover and re-frigerate any leftovers for up to three days, reheating before serving

# Brunch Eggs

*Time: 4 hours and 20 minutes / Serving 12*
*Net Carbs: 31g / 1.09oz (10%) Fat: 19g / 0.67oz (29%)*
*Protein: 19g / 0.67oz Kcal: 370*

## Ingredients:

- 850g / 30oz frozen shredded hash-brown potatoes
- 16 eggs
- 425g / 15oz black beans, drained and rinsed
- 240ml / 1 cup half and half
- ½ teaspoon salt
- ¼ teaspoon pepper
- 2 tablespoons butter or margarine
- 305g / 10 ¾oz condensed cream of mushroom soup
- 230g / 8oz shredded Colby-Monterey Jack cheese blend
- 230g / 8oz salsa

## Instructions:

1. In a microwavable dish, microwave the potatoes on high for 3 minutes and 30 seconds to 4 minutes; stir once and continue until thawed

2. Stir beans into the mixture

3. With the back of a spoon, press the mixture of beans and potatoes in the bottom and approximately 2 to 3 inches up the sides of the slow cooker

4. In a large bowl, beat the eggs, the half and half, salt, and pepper with a wire whisk until combined well

5. In a non-stick skillet (10-inch) melt the butter on a medium heat

6. Add egg mixture; cook and stir occasionally until the eggs have almost set

7. Spoon half of the egg mixture into the potato-filled slow cooker

8. Top the layer of egg with half of the soup, the cheese, and the salsa; add the rest of the egg and repeat the step

9. Cover and cook for 3 to 4 hours on low

# Salted Caramel-Banana Cinnamon Casserole

*Time: 2 hours and 20 minutes / Serving 8*
*Net Carbs: 78g / 2.75oz (26%) Fat: 12g / 0.42oz (19%)*
*Protein: 5g / 0.18oz Kcal: 370*

## Ingredients:

- 🍽 115g / 4oz cream cheese, cubed
- 🍽 350g / 1 cup salted caramel sauce
- 🍽 60g / ¼ cup milk
- 🍽 500g / 17.5oz Pillsbury™ Grands! refrigerated cinnamon rolls with icing
- 🍽 4 firm medium-sized bananas

## Instructions:

1. Spray a 6-quart slow cooker with a cooking spray of your choice

2. In a large microwavable bowl, microwave cream cheese, 264g / ¾ cup of salted caramel and the milk without a cover on high for 1 to 2 minutes; whisk every 30 seconds until the cream cheese cubes have combined

3. Separate the dough into 5 rolls – leave the icing in the refrigerator

4. Cut each of the rolls into 8 pieces and stir the pieces into the cream cheese mix until all are well coated

5. Move this mixture into the slow cooker

6. Cover the mix with a large kitchen towel and place the slow cooker lid on top of the towel – this will prevent the condensation dripping onto the rolls during cooking

7. Cook on low for 1 hour 45 minutes to 2 hours 30 minutes, rotating the insert 180 degrees after one hour; keep an eye on the casserole towards the end of cooking so as not to overcook

8. Once golden brown and the dough is baked through in the centre, it is done

9. Leave to stand for 10 minutes

10. In a small microwavable bowl, place icing and remaining salted caramel and heat on high for 10-15 seconds or until warm, stirring until blended

11. Top the casserole with the bananas, chopped, and the icing

# Ham and Swiss Quiche

*Time: 3 hours and 35 minutes / Serving 6*
*Net Carbs: 36g / 1.27oz Fat: 48g / 1.69oz*
*Protein: 23g / 0.81oz Kcal: 660*

## Ingredients:

- 🍽 1 box Pillsbury™ refrigerated pie crusts, softened as directed on the box
- 🍽 250g / 8oz shredded Swiss cheese
- 🍽 230g / 1 cup chopped lean cooked ham
- 🍽 4 green onions, chopped
- 🍽 240g / 1 cup whipping cream
- 🍽 ¼ teaspoon salt
- 🍽 ¼ teaspoon pepper
- 🍽 1/8 teaspoon ground nutmeg
- 🍽 If desired: pear or grape tomatoes and additional sliced green onions

## Instructions:

1. With a cooking spray of your choice, spray a 5- or 6-quart slow cooker to prevent sticking

2. Remove the pie crusts and cut in half; put 3 of the pie crust halves in the bottom and press them 2 inches up the sides of the slow cooker

3. Cover and cook on high heat for 1 hour 30 minutes

4. Sprinkle 4 oz Swiss cheese, the ham, and onions over crust

5. In a medium bowl, beat the eggs, whipping cream, salt, pepper, and nutmeg with a whisk

6. Pour this mixture over the filled crust in the slow cooker, sprinkle with remaining cheese

7. Cover and cook on a high heat for a further 1 hour 30 minutes or until filling is set in the crust

8. Uncover and leave to stand for 5 minutes before serving

9. Cut quiche into wedge and serve, garnished with tomatoes and additional green onions (optional)

# Perfect Sausage Breakfast Casserole

*Time: 4 hours and 55 minutes / Serving 8*
*Net Carbs: 19g / 0.56oz (6%) Fat: 37g / 1.31oz (57%)*
*Protein: 29g / 1.02oz Kcal: 530*

## Ingredients:

- 450g / 1lb bulk chorizo sausage or sweet Italian sausages
- 8 eggs
- 240ml / 1 cup milk
- 130g / 4.5oz chopped green chillies
- 230g / 8oz shredded Colby-Monterey Jack cheese blend
- 1 red bell pepper, chopped
- 9 soft corn tortillas
- 230g / 8oz salsa

## Instructions:

1. On a medium-high heat, cook the sausages in a 10-inch skillet for approximately 5 to 7 minutes, turning occasionally until they are no longer pink; drain and set to one side

2. In a medium bowl, beat the eggs, milk, and green chillies together with whisk; reserve ¾ cup of cheese and 2 tablespoons of chopped bell pepper for topping

3. Line a 5- or 6-quart slot cooker with foil folded into thirds, and spray the foil with a cooking spray

4. Place 3 tortillas onto the foil in the bottom of the slow cooker; layer half of the sausage and half of the remaining bell pepper and cheese

5. Top with the remaining three tortillas and pour the egg mixture over the slow cooker

6. Cover and cook on a low heat for 4 to 5 hours, or if you are in a hurry, on a high setting for 2 or 3 hours

7. Sprinkle the reserved chopped bell pepper and grated cheese, cover and cook for 5 minutes longer or until the cheese is melted

8. Remove the foil and serve with salsa

Note: Top with jalapeno chillies for an added heat flair!

# People-pleasing Scrambled eggs

*Time: 2 hours and 25 minutes / Serving 12*
*Net Carbs: 5g / 0.17oz (2%) Fat: 20g / 0.71oz (31%)*
*Protein: 20g / 0.71oz Kcal: 280*

## Ingredients:

- 12 eggs
- ½ teaspoon salt
- ½ teaspoon pepper
- 240g / 1 cup half and half
- 460g / 2 cups diced cooked ham
- 1 tablespoon butter or margarine
- 8 green onions, diced
- 1 small red bell pepper, diced
- 115g / 4oz shredded Cheddar cheese

## Instructions:

1. Spray 4- or 5-quart slow cooker with a cooking spray of your choice
2. In the cooker beat the salt and pepper together with the eggs and half and half with an electronic mixer on medium speed until the mixture is smooth
3. Sprinkle the ham into the mixture
4. Cover and cook on high heat setting for 1 hour, stirring after the first 30 minutes
5. Melt butter over medium heat in a 10-inch skillet; add the diced green onions and bell peppers; cook for about 5 minutes and stir occasionally
6. Stir the pepper mix and cheese into the eggs and serve immediately, or reduce the heat to low and hold for up to 1 hour before serving

Note: Roll the eggs and some salsa into a flour tortilla for a filling breakfast burrito!

# Turtle Monkey Bread

*Time: 2 hours and 35 minutes / Serving 12*
*Net Carbs: 37g / 1.31oz (12%) Fat: 19g / 0.67oz (29%)*
*Protein: 3g / 0.11oz Kcal: 330*

## Ingredients:

- 🍽 154g / 2/3 cup brown sugar
- 🍽 120g / ½ cup butter
- 🍽 56g / ¼ cup granulated sugar
- 🍽 470g / 16.3oz Refrigerated buttermilk biscuits
- 🍽 84g / ¾ cup pecans, halved
- 🍽 2 tablespoons whipping cream
- 🍽 50g / 1/3 cup milk chocolate chips

## Instructions:

1. Spray a 4 ½ - or 5-quart slow cooker with a cooking spray of your choice

2. In a microwavable cup, mix together brown sugar and butter and microwave on a high setting for 1 to 2 minutes, stirring every 30 seconds until the mixture is boiling and smooth

3. In a large plastic bag, place the sugar; separate the biscuits and cut into quarters – add to the bag with the sugar and shake to coat

4. Sprinkle 1/3 of the pecans into the slow cooker and top with half of the biscuit mixture; pour 1/3 of the butter mixture over the biscuits

5. Repeat the above steps until all are used

6. Cover and cook the bread on a high heat for 1 ½ to 2 hours until the knife comes out clean when inserted

7. Turn off the cooker and let the bread stand for 10 minutes

8. Once cooled, run a knife around the edge of cooker; turn bread upside down and serve on a heatproof plate

9. In a saucepan, heat the cream to just boiling; stir in the chocolate chips and heat until melted

10. Drizzle the chocolate sauce over monkey bread and serve warm

Note: You can swap the chocolate drizzle for ¼ cup hot fudge topping for a sweeter treat.

# Lunch

# Cheesy Potato Soup

*Time: 8 hours 50 minutes / Serving 6*
*Net Carbs: 12% (35g / 1.23oz) Fat: 19% (12g / 0.42oz)*
*Protein: 11g / 0.39oz Kcal: 300*

## Ingredients:

- 910g / 2lbs chicken broth
- 255g / 1 ½ cups chopped onions
- 5 medium diced and peeled russet potatoes
- 3 tablespoons corn-starch
- 230g / 8oz shredded American cheese
- 4 medium green onions, sliced

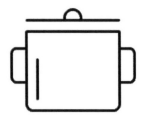

## Instructions:

1. Spray the inside of a 3 ½- to 4-quart slow cooker with a cooking spray of your choice

2. Reserve ¼ cup broth in a small bowl; cover this and leave it in your refrigerator

3. Mix onions, potatoes, and the remaining broth into the slow cooker

4. Cover and leave to cook on a low setting for 8 hours

5. After 8 hours, increase the setting to high

6. In a small bowl, beat together the corn-starch and remaining reserved broth until smooth

7. Add this to the cooker and stir in

8. Cover the slow cooker and heat to simmering and cook for a further 10 to 15 minutes or until the soup has thickened

9. Stir in the cheese until it has thoroughly melted

10. Dish out soup and sprinkle with green onions to serve

Note: Processed cheese is guaranteed to melt well, but for a healthy alternative nutty Swiss or smoky Monterey Jack will melt just as well! This soup can be stored for up to three days in the refrigerator if in tightly sealed containers!

# Mexican Pork-Filled Burrito Bowls

*Time: 7 hours / Serving 8*
*Net Carbs: 39g / 1.37oz (13%) Fat: 21g / 0.74oz (32%)*
*Protein: 39g / 1.37oz Kcal: 500*

## Ingredients:

- 1 large sweet onion, slice
- 2 tablespoons taco seasoning mix
- 1.4kg / 3lbs boneless pork shoulder
- 285g / 10oz red enchilada sauce
- 130g / 4.5oz chopped green chillies
- ½ teaspoon salt
- 1.1kg / 6 cups rice, cooked
- 340g / 2 cups shredded lettuce
- If desired: Salsa, shredded Mexican cheese blend and fresh cilantro, chopped

## Instructions:

1. Spray a 5-quart slow cooker with a cooking spray of your choice and add the onions

2. Sprinkle the taco seasoning over the pork shoulder and rub it in; place the seasoned pork in the cooker and top with the enchiladas sauce

3. Cover and cook on a high setting for 5 to 6 hours or until the pork is tender

4. Remove the pork from the slow cooker and shred the meat with two forks, discarding the fat

5. Place shredded pork in a large bowl

6. Strain the sauce and add, to the pork, 1 cup strained sauce, chillies, and salt; stir thoroughly

7. Spoon ¾ cup of rice into each bowl and top with ½ cup of pork and ¼ cup of lettuce

8. Garnish with additional toppings if desired and serve

Note: Cover and refrigerate leftovers; serve within 3 days.

# Dump-it-all-in Beef Stew

*Time: 5 hours 5 minutes / Serving 6*
*Net Carbs: 27g / 0.95oz Fat: 16g / 0.56oz*
*Protein: 31g / 1.09oz Kcal: 380*

## Ingredients:

- 910g / 2lbs beef stewing meat (chopped from the supermarket)
- 45g / 1.5oz beef stew seasoning mix
- 340g / 12oz frozen vegetables (preferably one with onions)
- 400g / 14oz yellow potatoes
- 230g / 8oz baby carrots
- 910ml / 32oz beef broth
- 30g / ¼ cup of all-purpose flour

## Instructions:

1. Spray your slow cooker with a cooking spray of your choice

2. Into the slow cooker, put the beef stew meat, the beef stew seasoning mix, the frozen mixed vegetables, the baby carrots, the potatoes, and the beef broth; stir well to combine

3. Cover this and cook on a high setting for 5 to 6 hours, or on a low setting for 8 to 10 hours if cooking overnight

4. Before serving, remove ½ cup of stew broth from the slow cooker and add to a small bowl; beat with the flour with a whisk until the mixture is smooth

5. Add flour mix back into the stew and mix until stew has thickened

Note: If you cannot find any beef stew seasoning, use a brown gravy mix as an equivalent; make sure to use the same amount.

# Chilli Verde

*Time: 6 hours 50 minutes / Serving 4*
*Net Carbs: 29g / 1.02oz (10%) Fat: 17g / 0.60oz (26%)*
*Protein: 39g / 1.38oz Kcal: 420*

## Ingredients:

- 1 teaspoon ground coriander
- ½ teaspoon ground cumin
- ½ teaspoon garlic salt
- 680g / 1 ½lb pork loin chops
- 455g / 1lb baby Dutch yellow potatoes
- 560ml / 20oz green enchilada sauce
- 1 ½ cups water
- If desired: crema Mexicana, chopped cilantro and fresh lime juice

## Instructions:

1. Spray the inside of your slow cooker with a cooking spray of your choice
2. Mix together the ground coriander, the ground cumin, and the garlic salt in a small bowl
3. Cut the pork into small pieces and rub with seasoning mixture; add the pork to the slow cooker
4. Rinse the potatoes and add to the slow cooker; add the green enchilada sauce and 1 ½ cups water – gently stir to mix water and sauce
5. Cover and cook on a high heat for 6 hours
6. Serve with toppings if desired

Note: For a thicker chilli, decrease the amount of water you add by 1 cup.

# Barbecue Ribs

*Time: 9 hours 40 minutes / Serving 4*
*Net Carbs: 58g / 2.05oz (18%) Fat: 58g / 2.05oz (89%)*
*Protein: 56g / 1.98oz Kcal: 980*

## Ingredients:

- 50g / ¼ cup brown sugar
- 1 teaspoon salt
- ½ teaspoon pepper
- 1.6kg / 3 ½lbs pork loin back ribs
- 1 medium onion, sliced
- 120ml / ½ cup Cola Carbonated beverage (Coke, Dr Pepper etc.)
- 500ml / 1 ½ cups barbecue sauce

## Instructions:

1. Spray the inside of a 4- or 5-quart slow cooker with a cooking spray of your choice

2. Mix together brown sugar, salt, and pepper; rub the mixture onto the ribs, making sure to coat both sides

3. Cut the ribs into sections of approximately 3 ribs

4. Layer the ribs and onions into the slow cooker; pour the cola beverage over the contents

5. Cover and cook on a low setting for 8 to 9 hours, or until the ribs are tender

6. Remove the ribs from slow cooker, discarding the liquid and onion slices

7. Set the over to broil and spray a broiler pan with a cooking spray of your choice

8. Pour barbecue sauce into a shallow bowl, dip ribs in sauce, coating both sides and place on the broiler pan, rib side against the pan

9. Broil the tops of the ribs 3 inches from the heat source for 3 to 4 minutes, until the sauce has just set; turn and broil for 3 to 5 minutes longer

10. Serve alongside the remaining barbecue sauce

Note: Store any leftovers in plastic food containers for up to three days.

# Butternut Squash Soup

*Time: 4 hours 55 minutes / Serving 6*
*Net Carbs: 19g / 0.67oz (6%) Fat: 8g / 0.28oz (12%)*
*Protein: 2g / 0.07oz Kcal: 150*

## Instructions:

- 🍽 910g / 2lbs butternut squash, peeled and cubed

- 🍽 1 large apple, peeled and chopped

- 🍽 85g / ½ cup chopped onion

- 🍽 1 teaspoon salt

- 🍽 1/8 teaspoon ground red cayenne pepper

- 🍽 230ml / 1 ¼ cup chicken broth

- 🍽 60g / ½ cup heavy whipping cream

## Instruction:

1. Spray a 4- or 5-quart slow cooker with a cooking spray of your choice

2. Add all ingredients except the whipping cream

3. Cover and cook on a high heat for 4 to 5 hours

4. Let the mixture call for 5 minutes before blending in a blender; return all squash to the slow cooker once blended

5. Stir in whipping cream

6. Cover and cook on a high heat for a further five minutes, or until heated through

Note: For an added flavour stir in ½ teaspoon of ground cinnamon, chopped thyme or curry powder. Sprinkle a little cayenne pepper over the soup as a garnish.

Important!: Blending hot liquids is dangerous but can be done safely when removing the centre portion of your blender and covering with a kitchen towel instead – this prevents it from exploding.

# Buffalo-Ranch Chicken

*Time: 45 minutes / Serving 5*
*Net Carbs: 8g / 0.28oz (3%) Fat: 23g / 0.81oz (36%)*
*Protein: 44g / 1.55oz Kcal: 420*

## Ingredients:

- 🍽 800g / 1.8lb boneless skinless chicken thighs

- 🍽 30g / 1oz ranch dressing and seasoning mix

- 🍽 340g / 1 oz Buffalo wing sauce

## Instructions:

1. In a large bowl, toss the chicken and seasoning mix, making sure to coat it evenly

2. Spray a 4- or 5-quart slow cooker with your choice of cooking spray and add the coated chicken – top the chicken with the buffalo sauce

3. Cover and cook on a low heat setting for 4 to 5 hours or until the chicken is tender

4. Take the chicken out of the slow cooker and place into a bowl; shred the chicken using two forks

5. Put the shredded chicken back into the slow cooker and stir to coat evenly with the sauce

6. Serve warm

# Creamy Tuscan Chicken

*Time: 3 hours 35 minutes / Serving 4*
*Net Carbs: 13g / 0.46oz (4%) Fat: 45g / 1.58oz (69%)*
*Protein: 13g / 0.49oz Kcal: 620*

## Ingredients:

- 1 tablespoon butter
- 570g / 1.3lb boneless skinless chicken breasts
- 430g / 15oz Alfredo pasta sauce with roasted garlic
- 200g / 7oz sundried tomato strips, cut into thin strips
- 60g / ¼ cup grated Parmesan cheese
- 1 teaspoon Italian seasoning
- 130g / 1 cup chopped fresh spinach

## Instructions:

1. In a 12-inch non-stick skillet, over a medium-high heat, melt the butter; add the chicken breasts and cook for 3-5 minutes until browned

2. In a 3 ½- or 4-quart slow cooker, add the chicken

3. Mix the Alfredo sauce, sundried tomatoes, Italian seasoning, and Parmesan in a medium bowl until thoroughly combined

4. Pour over chicken in the slow cooker

5. Cook on a low heat for 3 to 4 hours

6. Stir in the spinach and cook for a further five minutes

7. Serve with linguine or rice, if desired

# Chicken Alfredo Stew

*Time: 6 hours 40 minutes / Serving 6*
*Net Carbs: 33g / 1.16oz (11%) Fat: 31g / 1.10oz (48%)*
*Protein: 30g / 1.06oz Kcal: 530*

## Ingredients:

- 460g / 16oz Alfredo pasta sauce
- 180ml / ¾ cup water
- ½ teaspoon dried basil
- ½ teaspoon salt
- 730g / 4 cups diced potatoes with onions (from a 20-oz bag)
- 570g / 1 ¼ lb boneless skinless chicken thighs, cut into strips
- 460g / 16oz frozen vegetable mix

## Instructions:

1. Mix together the pasta sauce, salt, water, and basil in a small bowl
2. Spray 3- or 4-quart slow cooker with your choice of cooking spray
3. In the cooker, layer half each of the potatoes, chicken strips, frozen vegetables, and pasta sauce; repeat
4. Cover the mix and cook on a low setting for 6 to 8 hours
5. Serve warm

Note: If you are a fan of garlic, try using the garlic-flavoured Alfredo pasta sauce

# Carolina-Style Pulled Pork

*Time: 8 hours 40 minutes / Serving 12*
*Net Carbs: 6g / 0.21oz (2%) Fat: 15g / 0.53oz (23%)*
*Protein: 20g / 0.71oz Kcal: 240*

## Ingredients:

- 145g / 2/3 cup yellow mustard
- 125ml / ½ cup soy sauce
- 100g / ½ cup brown sugar
- 3 tablespoons chilli powder
- ½ teaspoon garlic powder
- 1.4 to 1.8kg / 3 to 4lbs boneless pork shoulder
- 60ml / ¼ cup apple cider vinegar

## Instructions:

1. Spray a 5-quart or larger slow cooker with a cooking spray of your choice

2. In a medium bowl beat together the mustard, soy sauce, brown sugar, garlic powder, 2 teaspoons of salt, and chilli powder

3. Pour mix into slow cooker and add pork; turn meat to coat

4. Cover and cook on a low heat for 8 to 9 hours

5. Move the pork to a cutting board and allow to cool

6. Strain the sauce through a strainer or sieve and discard the solids in the strainer

7. Pour 1 ¼ cups of sauce into a small bowl and stir in the vinegar

8. When the pork has cooled and can be handled, shred between two forks, discarding fat and transfer the pork back to the slow cooker and pour the sauce and vinegar over

9. Toss to mix

Note: If you're a fan of spice, add 1 to 2 tablespoons of Sriracha sauce to the sauce. The remaining meat sauce can be combined with ¼ cup cider vinegar to make a coleslaw dressing.

# Dinner

# Chicken Parmesan Tortellini

*Time: 4 hours / Serving 6*
*Net Carbs: 12% (35g / 1.23oz) Fat: 33% (22g / 0.77oz)*
*Protein: 35g / 1.23oz Kcal: 480*

## Ingredients:

- 🍽 730g / 25.5oz tomato and basil pasta sauce
- 🍽 475ml / 2 cups chicken broth
- 🍽 1 teaspoon salt
- 🍽 460g / 1lb boneless and skinless chicken breasts
- 🍽 570g / 20oz cheese-filled tortellini
- 🍽 115g / 4oz shredded mozzarella
- 🍽 1 tablespoon butter
- 🍽 160g / ½ cup panko crispy breadcrumbs
- 🍽 57g / 2oz Parmesan cheese
- 🍽 If desired: fresh basil

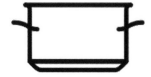

## Instructions:

1. Spray 4 ½- or 5-quart slow cooker with your choice of cooking spray; mix pasta sauce, broth, and salt in cooker

2. To the cooker, add the chicken breasts

3. Cover and cook on a low heat for 3 to 4 hours, until the juices of the chicken are clear

4. Remove chicken from the sauce and shred with two forks

5. Stir the tortellini into cooker; cover and cook on low heat for 15 minutes

6. Top the tortellini mixture with the shredded chicken

7. Top the shredded chicken with mozzarella cheese

8. Cover and cook for 10 to 15 minutes, or until the tortellini is tender and the cheese has melted

9. Melt the butter over a medium heat, in a 10-inch skillet and add the breadcrumbs; cook and stir for 2 to 5 minutes

10. Sprinkle over the mixture in the slow cooker, top with parmesan and basil and serve

Note: Dice the chicken instead of shredding for a chunkier consistency.

# Root Beer Chicken

*Time: 2 hours 35 minutes / Serving 8*
*Net Carbs: 25% (25g / 0.88oz) Fat: 8% (5g / 0.18oz)*
*Protein: 46.5% (32g / 1.13oz) Kcal: 270*

## Ingredients:

- 1.15kg / 2 ½lbs boneless skinless chicken breast
- Salt and Pepper
- 500g / 1 ½ cups barbecue sauce
- 240ml / 1 cup root beer

## Instructions:

1. Spray a slow cooker with cooking spray of your choice
2. Season the chicken breasts on either side with salt and pepper and place into the slow cooker
3. Pour the barbecue sauce and root beer into the slow cooker and mix
4. Cover and cook on a high heat for two hours
5. Take the chicken from the slow cooker and place on a plate
6. Use two forks to shred and then place back into the slow cooker on the warming setting for a further 30 minutes
7. Serve, with burger buns if desired

# Hawaiian Pork Rice Bowls

*Time: 8 hours 20 minutes / Serving 6*
*Net Carbs: 18% (54g / 1.90oz) Fat: 41% (27g / 0.95oz)*
*Protein: 52g / 1.83oz Kcal: 670*

## Ingredients:

- 1.4kg / 3lbs boneless pork shoulder
- 2 teaspoons of liquid smoke
- 700g / 3 cups stir fry vegetables
- 1 tablespoon of coarse sea salt
- 1.1kg / 6 cups cooked white rice
- 150g / 1 cup chopped fresh pineapple
- 60ml / ¼ cup of teriyaki sauce
- 60g / 1/3 cup green onion, sliced

## Instructions:

1.  Spray a 5- and 6-quart slow cooker with cooking spray of your choice

2.  Place pork in a slow cooker; drizzle the liquid smoke over the top of pork and sprinkle with the salt

3.  Cover and cook on a low heat for 7 to 8 hours

4.  Transfer the pork to a large cutting board and leave to cool

5.  Shred pork with two forks when cool enough to handle; discard that fat and cartilage

6.  Strain the juices from the slow cooker

7.  Add ¾ cup of strained juices to the pork; cover and keep warm

8.  Heat ¼ cup water and the vegetable mixture over medium high heat in a 10-inch skillet

9.  Cover and steam for five minutes before adding the teriyaki sauce and continuing to cook for a further two minutes

10. Divide the rice, topping each with ¾ cup of the shredded pork, the teriyaki vegetables, pineapple, and green onion

11. For a fuller flavour, serve the rice bowl with additional teriyaki sauce

Note: Toasted sesame seeds are a nice addition to the rice bowls. Leftover pork is great in tacos.

# Taco Ground Beef

*Time: 8 hours 30 mins / Serving 16*
*Net Carbs: 8g / 0.28oz (3%) Fat: 9g / 0.32oz (14%)*
*Protein: 16g / 0.56oz Kcal: 180*

## Ingredients:

- 1.4kg / 3lbs lean ground beef
- 340g / 12oz frozen chopped onions, thawed
- 460g / 16oz medium or hot salsa
- 460g / 16oz refried beans
- 30g / 1oz taco seasoning mix
- 4 crunchy taco shells
- 230g / 8oz shredded 4-cheese blend

## Instructions:

1. Spray 5-quart slow cooker with a cooking spray of your choice
2. Break up the beef and place it on the bottom and up the sides of the slow cooker
3. Mix together the onions, beans, salsa and taco seasoning mix in a large bowl and mix place in the centre of the slow cooker
4. Cover and cook on a low heat for 8 hours
5. Drain the beef mixture through a strainer over a large bowl
6. Divide into portions and fill the tacos, topping with the cheese and any other toppings you want
7. Transfer remaining portions into freezer-proof containers and freeze for up to three months

Note: Save the strained liquid for a super flavourful braising liquid for your next pot roast!

# Orange Chicken

*Time: 2 hours 25 minutes / Serving 4*
*Net Carbs: 55g / 1.94oz (18%) Fat: 5g / 0.18oz (8%)*
*Protein: 35g / 1.23oz Kcal: 400*

## Ingredients:

- 160g / ½ cup sweet orange marmalade
- 1 tablespoon chilli garlic sauce
- 570g / 1.3lbs boneless skinless chicken breast, diced
- 2 tablespoons corn-starch
- 2 tablespoons soy sauce
- 2 tablespoons chopped cilantro
- 2 cups cooked white rice

## Instructions:

1. Spray 2 ½- to 3-quart slow cooker with a cooking spray of your choice

2. Into a small bowl, mix the marmalade and chilli garlic sauce

3. Add the marmalade mixture and the chicken breast into the slow cooker and mix thoroughly to coat the chicken with the mixture

4. Cover and cook on a low heat for 1 hour 30 minutes

5. Into a small bowl, mix corn-starch and soy sauce; stir this mix into the slow cooker mixture

6. Cover and cook on a high heat for 30 to 40 minutes, until the chicken is no longer pink in the centre and the sauce is bubbling at the edges; make sure the sauce is also a thicker consistency before serving

7. Remove from the slow cooker, sprinkle with cilantro and serve with rice

Note: Add additional chilli garlic sauce to spice up the heat

# Beef Bolognese

*Time: 5 hours / Serving 8*
*Net Carbs: 19g / 0.67oz (6%) Fat: 18g / 0.63oz (28%)*
*Protein: 22g / 0.78oz Kcal: 330*

## Ingredients:

- 910g / 2lbs lean ground beef
- 170g / 1 cup chopped onions
- 3 garlic cloves
- 90g / ½ cup finely chopped carrot
- 90g / ½ cup finely chopped celery
- 1 ½ teaspoons salt
- ½ teaspoon black pepper
- 1.6kg / 56oz crushed tomatoes with basil
- 120g / ½ cup heavy whipping cream

## Instructions:

1. Spray a 5-quart slow cooker with a cooking spray of your choice
2. In 12-inch skillet, cook the onion, garlic, beef, celery, carrot, salt and pepper on a medium-high heat for 6 to 7 minutes; stir frequently until the beef is thoroughly cooked
3. Drain the beef mixture and add to the slow cooker
4. Stir in tomatoes
5. Cover and cook on a low heat setting for 4 to 5 hours
6. Stir in whipping cream and cover and cook for a further 10 minutes
7. Serve with pasta of your choice
8. To freeze: Pour into freezer-proof Tupperware and keep for up to three months

# Cheesy Meatballs and Pasta

*Time: 4 hours 30 minutes / Serving 6*
*Net Carbs: 85g / 3oz (28%) Fat: 23g / 0.81oz (35%)*
*Protein: 42g / 1.48oz Kcal: 710*

## Ingredients:

- 🍽 680g / 1 ½ lb lean ground beef

- 🍽 60g / ½ cup breadcrumbs

- 🍽 2 tablespoons milk

- 🍽 1 egg, slightly beaten

- 🍽 Salt and pepper

- 🍽 5 mozzarella sticks, cut into small pieces

- 🍽 680g / 24oz tomato pasta sauce

- 🍽 460g / 16oz pasta

## Instructions:

1. In a large bowl, add beef, milk, breadcrumbs, eggs, salt and pepper; mix well with hands until combined

2. Shape mixture into small balls

3. With your finger, make a hole in the ball, ¾ of the way down the ball; place a piece of cheese in the hole and reroll the meatballs to cover the cheese

4. Repeat step three with all the balls

5. Spray a 3 ½- or 4-quart slow cooker with a cooking spray of your choice

6. Pour the pasta sauce into the cooker and place meatballs into the sauce

7. Cover and cook on a low heat for 4 hours

8. Approximately 25 minutes before the meatballs are done, cook the pasta as directed by the packet

Note: Add a teaspoon of garlic powder, onion powder and parsley flakes for a bigger flavour boost

# Italian Meatloaf

*Time: 5 hours 40 minutes / Serving 6*
*Net Carbs: 16g / 0.56oz (5%) Fat: 21g / 0.74oz (32%)*
*Protein: 31g / 1.09oz Kcal: 370*

## Ingredients:

- 🍽 680g / 1 ½lbs lean ground beef
- 🍽 2 roasted red bell pepper, finely chopped
- 🍽 80g / ¾ cup breadcrumbs
- 🍽 260g / 1 cup grated Parmesan cheese
- 🍽 2 eggs
- 🍽 240g / 1 cup marinara sauce

## Instructions:

1. Line the bottom and sides of the slow cooker with a large sheet of foil and lightly spray with a cooking spray of your choice

2. In a large bowl, stir the beef, chopped red bell peppers, breadcrumbs, cheese and eggs

3. Mix the combination thoroughly with clean hands and shape into a loaf; place this loaf into the slow cooker

4. Cover and cook on low heat for 5 to 6 hours

5. Uncover the loaf and pour the marinara sauce evenly over the meatloaf

6. Cover and cook for a further 15 minutes longer or until the sauce has been heated

7. Using the sides of the foil, remove the meatloaf from the slow cooker and allow to stand for 10 minutes

8. Serve

Note: You can heat the marinara in a saucepan if you are in a rush

# 3-Ingredient Italian Chicken

*Time: 4 hours 20 minutes / Serving 6*
*Net Carbs: 14g / 0.49oz (5%) Fat: 9g / 0.32oz (14%)*
*Protein: 33g / 1.16oz Kcal: 270*

## Ingredients:

- 🍽 910g / 2lbs boneless skinless chicken thighs
- 🍽 680g / 24oz marinara pasta sauce – choose your favourite!
- 🍽 1 medium red bell pepper, diced

## Instructions:

1. Spray a 3 ½- or 4-quart slow cooker with a cooking spray of your choice
2. Place chicken in the slow cooker
3. Put the bell peppers and pasta sauce on top of the chicken
4. Cover and cook on a low heat for 4 to 5 hours
5. Serve with pasta or rice

Note: Top with grated or shredded Parmesan cheese to give a little something extra to the dish. Chopped parsley can also help with giving added flavour.

# Beefy Enchilada Stack

*Time: 3 hours 5 minutes / Serving 8*
*Net Carbs: 38g / 1.34oz (13%) Fat: 22g / 0.78oz (33%)*
*Protein: 26g / 0.92oz Kcal: 450*

## Ingredients:

- 460g / 1lb ground beef
- 215g / 1 ¼ cups chopped onions
- 2 medium poblano chillies, seeded and chopped
- 2 cloves of garlic, finely chopped
- 570g / 20oz enchilada sauce
- 30g / 1oz taco seasoning
- 170g / 1 cup frozen corn
- 425g / 15oz black beans, drained and rinsed
- 10 soft corn tortillas
- 340g / 12oz shredded Cheddar cheese
- 35g / ¼ cup chopped fresh cilantro

## Instructions:

1. Line the bottom and sides of the slow cooker with a large sheet of foil and lightly spray with a cooking spray of your choice

2. In a large bowl, stir the beef, roasted red bell peppers, breadcrumbs, cheese and eggs

3. Using clean hands, mix thoroughly and shape into a loaf; place the loaf into the slow cooker

4. Cover and cook on low heat for 5 to 6 hours

5. Uncover the loaf and pour the marinara sauce evenly over the meatloaf

6. Cover and cook for a further 15 minutes longer or until the sauce has been heated

7. Using the sides of the foil, remove the meatloaf and allow to stand for 10 minutes before serving

Note: You can heat the marinara in a saucepan if you are in a rush

# Desserts

# Chocolate-Butterscotch Lava Cake

*Time: 5 hours 15 minutes / Serving 12*
*Net Carbs: 70.5g / 2.49oz Fat: 23.5g / 0.83oz*
*Protein: 8g / 0.28oz Kcal: 534*

## Ingredients:

- 1 box of dark chocolate cake mix
- 1 box of chocolate instant pudding and pie filling mix
- 1 cup sour cream
- 1/3 cup butter
- 1 teaspoon vanilla
- 3 ¼ cups milk
- 3 eggs
- 230g / 8oz toffee bits
- 1 box of butterscotch instant pudding and pie filling mix
- 230g / 8oz whipped topping

## Instructions:

1. Spray a 5-quart slow cooker with a cooking spray of your choice

2. In a large bowl, mix the cake mix, chocolate pudding mix, sour cream, vanilla, butter, one 1 ¼ cups of the milk and the eggs with electric mixer on a medium speed for two minutes, making sure to scape the sides as needed

3. Stir in 1 cup of the toffee bits

4. Pour the batter into the slow cooker

5. In a saucepan, heat the remaining two cups of milk over a medium heat for approximately 3-5 minutes until bubbling, stirring frequently to avoid it burning on the bottom

6. Sprinkle in the butterscotch pudding mix to the top of the batter in slow cooker; pour the hot milk on top of this

7. Cover and cook on a low setting for 4 hours 30 minutes

8. Turn off the slow cooker

9. Let stand for 15 minutes before garnishing with whipped topping and remaining toffee bits

Note: This lava cake is good with ice cream as well!

# Rice Pudding

*Time: 3 hours 50 minutes / Serving 12*
*Net Carbs: 27g / 0.95oz (9%) Fat: 3g / 0.11oz (4%)*
*Protein: 3g / 0.11oz Kcal: 700*

## Ingredients:

- 205g / 1 ½ cups uncooked long grain white rice (cannot be instant or precooked)
- 710ml / 3 cups water
- 100g / ½ cup sugar
- 1 teaspoon ground cinnamon
- 2 tablespoons butter, melted
- 680g / 24oz evaporated milk
- 1 teaspoon vanilla

## Instructions:

1. Spray the inside of a 3 ½-quart slow cooker with your choice of cooking spray

2. In a saucepan, heat rice and water to boiling over medium heat

3. Cover and reduce the heat to low and cook for 20-25 minutes; make sure that the rice is tender and all liquid absorbed

4. Add rice slow cooker and stir in the remaining ingredients until the entirety is well mixed

5. Cover and cook on a low heat for 2 hours; remove the cover and stir

6. Cover and cook for a further 30 to 40 minutes longer

7. Turn off the heat, remove cover and stir; leave for 15 minutes before serving

8. Serve warm with a topping of your choice

Note: Adding a dash of cinnamon or handful of chopped walnuts will really spice up this dish.

# Peaches and Cream Tapioca

*Time: 4 hours 20 minutes / Serving 8*
*Net Carbs: 52g / 1.83oz Fat: 13g / 0.46oz*
*Protein: 4g / 0.14oz Kcal: 330*

## Ingredients:

- 910g / 2lbs fresh or defrosted peach slices
- 3 tablespoons quick-cooking tapioca
- 150g / ¾ cup packed brown sugar
- 240g / 2 cups granola
- 1/8 teaspoon ground nutmeg
- 240g / 1 cup whipping cream
- ½ cup peach nectar
- 1/8 teaspoon salt
- If desired: whipped topping

## Instructions:

1. Spray a 3 ½-quart slow cooker with a cooking spray of your choice
2. Into the slow cooker put the peaches, tapioca, salt, nutmeg, sugar, whipping cream and peach nectar; stir to mix
3. Cover and cook on a low heat for 4 hours
4. Stir well and spoon into dessert dishes, topping with ¼ cup of granola and whipped topping

# Praline Apple Crisp

*Time: 4 hours 50 minutes / Serving 10*
*Net Carbs: 30g / 1.06oz (10%) Fat: 17g / 0.60oz (27%)*
*Protein: 2g / 0.07oz Kcal: 280*

## Ingredients:

- 6 medium crisp tart apples (either Granny Smith or Braeburn), peeled and cut into thick slices
- 1 teaspoon ground cinnamon
- 55g / ½ cup quick cooking oats
- 1/3 cup brown sugar
- 35g / ¼ cup all-purpose flour
- 60g / ½ cup chopped pecan
- 55g / ½ cup toffee bits
- If desired: ice cream

## Instructions:

1. Spray 3- or 4-quart slow cooker with a cooking spray of your choice
2. In a large bowl, mix together the apples and cinnamon, making sure all are coated
3. Place the apple mix in the slow cooker
4. In a medium bowl, mix the oats, brown sugar, flour, and butter together with a fork until crumbly
5. Stir in pecans and toffee bits
6. Sprinkle the crumble mixture over the apples evenly
7. Cover and cook on a low setting for 4 to 6 hours and serve with ice cream or an alternative side

# Pumpkin Swirl Cheesecake

*Time: 10 hours 40 minutes / Serving 8*
*Net Carbs: 41g / 1.45oz (43%) Fat: 28g / 0.99oz (14%)*
*Protein: 6g / 0.21oz Kcal: 440*

## Ingredients:

Crust:

- 140g / 1 ¼ cups graham cracker crumbs
- 70g / 1/3 cup sugar
- 60g / ¼ cup butter, melted

Cheesecake:

- 460g / 16oz cream cheese, softened
- 150g / ¾ cup sugar
- 2 eggs
- 120g / ½ cup canned pumpkin (not pie mix)
- ½ teaspoon pumpkin pie spice

## Instructions:

1. Lightly Spray an 8-inch pan with a cooking spray of your choice. In a small bowl, mix the crust ingredients together

2. Press the mixture into the pan on the bottom and an inch up the sides of the pan

3. In a large bowl, beat cream cheese with an electronic mixer on a medium speed until smooth

4. Gradually add sugar, and beat in the eggs one by one, on a low speed, until blended together

5. Spoon ¾ of the mixture into the pan and spread evenly

6. Beat the pumpkin and pumpkin spice into the remaining cream cheese mix and whisk smooth

7. Spoon into pan and mix with a knife to create a pattern on the top

8. Place a small ovenproof bowl in the bottom of a 6- or 7-quart round slow cooker; place a plate on top of this bowl

9. Set the cheesecake on the place, place layers of paper towels on the top before covering and sealing with a lid

10. Cook on a high heat setting for 3 hours without removing the lid

11. Turn off the slow cooker and leave to stand for one hour before touching

12. Remove the cover and transfer the cheesecake to the refrigerator; leave there for at least 6 hours before serving but no longer than 24 hours

Note: Use gingersnap cookies instead of graham cracker crumbs for a festive treat!

# Keto Breakfast Bonus

# Breakfast Casserole

*Time: 1 ¾ hours / Serving 4*
*Net Carbs: 5% (6.1g / 0.22oz) Fiber: 0.9% (2.1g / 0.007oz) Fat: 64.1% (9.8g / 0.54oz)*
*Protein: 30% (22.9g / 0.82oz) Kcal: 313*

## Ingredients:

- 6 large eggs
- 90g / 3.2oz bacon slices
- 30g / 1.1oz chopped shallots
- 75g / 2.7oz chopped red bell pepper
- 70g / 2.5oz chopped white mushrooms
- 160g / 5.6oz of kale, shredded finely
- 15g / 0.5oz butter or ghee
- 90g / 3.2oz Parmesan cheese shredded - or substitute for a cheese of choice
- Salt and pepper - to season

## Instructions:

1. Chop the kale into small pieces, making sure to remove the stems

2. Cook bacon until crispy and then add in the red pepper, mushroom and shallot, sauté until soft

3. Toss in the kale and turn off the heat, so that the kale wilts

4. Beat the eggs, and season with the salt and pepper

5. Turn your slow cooker onto high heat and put the butter inside the pot to melt; once melted brush the sides of the slow cooker and up the sides to make sure nothing can stick

6. To the slow cooker, add the sautéed vegetables

7. Sprinkle the cheese over the vegetables then add the seasoned egg mix

8. Thoroughly stir the ingredients to mix and cook at high setting for 2 hours or at a low heat for 6 hours

# Breakfast Enchiladas

*Time: 25 minutes / Serving 4*
*Net Carbs: 6.08g / 0.21oz Fat: 42.55g / 1.50oz*
*Protein: 27.3g / 0.96oz Kcal: 525*

## Ingredients:

- 6 large eggs
- 60ml / ¼ cup heavy whipping cream
- ½ tsp / 2.5 ml salt
- ½ tsp / 2.5 ml garlic powder
- ½ tsp / 2.5 ml chili powder
- ¼ tsp / 1.25 ml black pepper
- 230g / 8oz ground sausage
- 180ml / ¾ cup enchilada sauce
- 375ml / 1½ cups shredded cheddar cheese

## Instructions:

1. Turn your oven on to 400F and preheat a small skillet
2. Add the cream, salt, chilli, eggs, garlic powder, and black pepper in a bowl and whisk together
3. Pour 60ml / ¼ cup portions of the mixture into the pan and cover, cooked for 4 minutes, and then repeat with the other batter to create the rest of the chips
4. Add the cheese and sausage to your tortilla roll and place them in the slow cooker
5. Making sure to cover all the egg, pour the enchilada sauce onto the mix
6. Top with the last of the cheese and cook on a high heat for 15 minutes

# Keto Lunch Bonus

# Lemon-Garlic Chicken

*Time: 4 hours / Serving 4*
*Net Carbs: 2.6% (7.9g / 0.28oz) Fiber: 1.4% (0.4g / 0.05oz) Fat: 25.8% (16.8g / 0.6oz)*
*Protein: 126.7% (63.4g / 224oz) Kcal: 447*

## Ingredients:

- 🍲 225g / 1 cup of chicken broth (low sodium)
- 🍲 125ml / ½ a cup of squeezed lemon juice
- 🍲 1 tbsp / 15ml of olive oil
- 🍲 4 skinless and boneless chicken breasts
- 🍲 ¼ tsp / 1.25ml of ground pepper black
- 🍲 ½ tsp / 2.5ml of kosher salt
- 🍲 8 garlic cloves
- 🍲 2 tbsp / 30ml of unsalted butter
- 🍲 2 tbsp / 30ml of flour

## Instructions:

1. Begin by heating 1 tbsp / 15ml of the oil until it shines

2. With the salt and pepper, season chicken breasts on either side

3. Put the chicken into the pan and keep turning it until it is brown (this should take about 5 minutes)

4. Remove the seared chicken and place into the slow cooker

5. Add the broth, garlic, and lemon juice to the slow cooker

6. Cover and cook on a low heat for 3 – 4 hours until the chicken is cooked thoroughly; make sure the juices run clear and the chicken is tender too

7. Mix the 2 tbsp / 30ml butter and flour in a small bowl and rub with your fingers until combined

8. Put the chicken onto plates

9. Pour the liquid out of the slow cooker into a small pan and bring to boil, add the butter mix, and whisk continually until it creates a sauce

10. Pour the liquid over the chicken and enjoy

# Pork Tenderloin

*Time: 4 hours / Serving 8*
*Net Carbs: 0% (0g / 0.00oz) Fat: 33% (7g / 0.25oz)*
*Protein: 64% (23g / 0.81oz) Kcal: 169*

## Ingredients:

- 0.9-1.3kg / 2-2.9lbs pork tenderloin
- 4 garlic cloves chopped
- Juice of one lemon
- 2 tbsp / 30ml olive oil
- 1 tsp / 5ml salt
- 1 tsp / 5ml pepper
- ½-1 tsp / 2.5ml-5ml gravy thickening

## Instructions:

1. Place the pork tenderloin into the slow cooker
2. Add the garlic, olive oil, pepper, salt and lemon juice to the pork and mix
3. Cover and cook for 3 – 4 hours
4. Remove the pork from the slow cooker and sprinkle gravy thickener into the remaining liquid and then whisk
5. Once the gravy has thickened, cut the pork and place on plates
6. Serve with gravy

# Keto Dinner Bonus

# Slow Salmon

*Time: 2 hours / Serving 6*
*Net Carbs: 2.1% (6.29g / 0.22oz) Fiber: 0.9% (0.2g / 0.007oz) Fat: 23.5% (15.3g / 0.54oz)*
*Protein: 46.5% (23.3g / 0.82oz) Kcal: 261*

## Ingredients:

- 450-900g / 1-2lbs salmon fillets with skin on
- 225g-340g / 1-1 ½ cups of chosen liquid (broth, cider, water etc.)
- Salt
- Fresh black pepper
- Spices (if desired)
- Sliced lemon (if desired)
- Sliced aromatic vegetables, onions, celery etc. (if desired)

## Instructions:

1. Begin by cutting the salmon into a number of fillets

2. Season the fillets with fresh salt and pepper on the flesh side

3. Sprinkle any other spices if you have chosen to use them; use your fingers to rub everything in – this allows for good flavour in the meat

4. Line your slow cooker with a square of foil or parchment and place into the slow cooker

5. Into the bottom of the slow cooker add the vegetables and spices if you're adding them

6. If required, place a layer of lemons – this will add flavour

7. Place your initial layer of salmon, making sure to put the larger skin side down

8. Add another layer complete with further lemon and vegetables

9. Add your chosen liquid to your slow cooker with the lemon and salmon combination

10. Cover and cook on a low heat for 1 to 2 hours

11. Remove the salmon from the slow cooker and serve immediately or cool and refrigerate

12. The liquid in the slow cooker can be thrown away

# Chili Steak

*Time: 6 hours / Serving 12*
*Net Carbs: 4.79g / 0.17oz Fat: 37.26g / 1.31oz*
*Protein: 16g / 0.56oz Kcal: 478*

## Ingredients:

- 1.2kg / 2 ½ lbs steak, in 1" cubes
- 1 tbsp / 15ml of ancho chili powder
- ½ tsp / 2.5ml ground cumin
- ½ tsp / 2.5ml salt
- ¼ tsp / 1.25 ml of ground cayenne pepper
- ¼ tsp / 1.25 ml of ground black pepper
- ½ cup sliced leeks
- 500ml / 2 cups canned tomatoes, include the juice
- 250ml / 1 cup of chicken or beef stock

## Instructions:

1. Place all the ingredients into your slow cooker
2. Stir until well mixed and cook on a high heat for approximately 6 hours or until a point where the steak has softened
3. With a fork, break up any of the tomatoes that are still whole
4. Shred the steak if needed or slice to serve
5. Serve and enjoy

# *Day One*

*Breakfast: Casserole Tex-Mex-Style (See page 24)*
*Lunch: Dump-It-All-In Beef Stew (See page 46)*
*Dinner: Sweet and Sour Chicken*
*Time: 10 hours 50 minutes / Serving 6*
*Net Carbs: 84g / 3oz (28%) Fat: 12g / 0.4oz (18%)*
*Protein: 32g / 1.1oz Kcal: 570*

## Ingredients:

- 900g / 2lbs boneless, skinless chicken thighs, cut into 1 ½ inch sections
- 450g / 16oz broccoli, carrots and water chestnuts combined
- 320g / 11.5oz sweet and sour sauce
- 3 cups water
- 3 cups uncooked instant rice

## Instructions:

1. Spray the inside of a 3 ½- to 4-quart slow cooker with a cooking spray of your choice

2. Combine the chicken and the sauce and stir gently to mix together

3. Cover and cook this for 8 to 10 hours on a low setting, or until the chicken is no longer pink inside

4. 15 minutes before serving, turn the slow cooker to a high heat and add the vegetables

5. Cook the rice as directed on the packaging

6. Serve the chicken and vegetable mix over the rice

Note: Thighs are recommended for this recipe as chicken breast tends to dry out in the slow cooker

# Day Two

*Breakfast: Bacon, Egg and Cheese Casserole*
*Time: 5 hours and 40 minutes / Serving 8*
*Net Carbs: 41g /1.47oz (14%) Fat: 33g /1.16oz (51%)*
*Protein: 30g /1.06oz Kcal: 580*

## Ingredients:

- 🍽 625g / 22oz French bread
- 🍽 12 eggs
- 🍽 230g / 8oz grated Cheddar Cheese
- 🍽 2 cups half and half
- 🍽 450g / 1lb bacon, thickly sliced, cooked, and chopped

## Instructions:

1. Cut your bread so that you have 1/2-inch cubes
2. Line side of your slow cooker with foil, which you have folded into thirds
3. Spray the foil with your cooking spray
4. Beat the eggs and half-and-half in a large bowl
5. Stir the cheese and bacon, then add the bread cubes
6. Spoon your mixture into slow cooker
7. Cover and cook for 4 – 5 hours on a low setting
8. Once cooked sprinkle the rest of the cheese over the casserole and cook for a further 10 minutes or until the cheese has melted
9. Remove the foil, serve, and enjoy

*Lunch: Chilli Verde (See page 47)*
*Dinner: Hawaiian Pork Rice Bowls (See page 61)*

# Day Three

*Breakfast: People-pleasing Scrambled Eggs (See page 37)*
*Lunch: Bacon & Corn Slow Cooked Chowder*
*Time: 4 hours 30 minutes / Serving 8*
*Net Carbs: 32g /1.13oz (11%) Fat: 18g / 0.53oz (27%)*
*Protein: 15g / 1.98oz Kcal: 350*

## Ingredients:

- 450g / 16oz red potatoes cut into 1-inch cubes
- ½ cup onion chopped
- 2 bags (340g / 12oz each) frozen kernel corn
- 3 cups Progresso™ chicken broth (from 907g / 32oz carton)
- 1 tsp salt
- ½ tsp ground pepper
- 2 cups half-and-half
- 2 tbsps. corn-starch
- 230g / 8oz bacon, cooked until crisp then crumbled

## Instructions:

1. Mix the onion, corn, potatoes, broth and salt and pepper and place in the slow cooker

2. Cover and cook on high until the potatoes are softened, on a high heat 3 - 4 hours

3. Beat the half-and-half with the corn-starch until smooth

4. Stir the bacon and half-and-half mixture into the slow cooker

5. Cover and cool for a further 15 minutes

6. Serve

*Dinner: Chicken Alfredo Stew (See page 54)*

# Day Four

*Breakfast: Ham and Swiss Quiche (See page 33)*
*Lunch: Carolina-Style Pulled Pork (See page 55)*
*Dinner: Chicken Parmesan Tortellini (See page 58)*
*Dessert: Slow Apple Crisp*
*Time: 2 hours 45 minutes / Serving 6*
*Net Carbs: 79g /2.79oz (26%) Fat: 16g / 0.56oz (25%)*
*Protein: 3g /0.10oz Kcal: 470*

## Ingredients:

- 6 small peeled red apples cut into ½" slices
- ½ cup of granulated sugar

- 2 tbsp all-purpose flour
- 1 tsp ground cinnamon

Topping

- ½ cup flour (all-purpose)
- ½ cup oats (old-fashioned)
- ¾ cup brown sugar
- ¼ tsp salt
- ½ cup butter cut into 8 pieces

## Instructions:

1. In a large bowl put the sliced apple granulated sugar, 2 tbsp of flour and the cinnamon then mix until the apple is coated

2. Spray your slow cooker and add the apple mixture

3. Mix the flour, oats, salt, and brown sugar and stir until combined

4. Cut the butter and add to the mixture until it is crumbly

5. Sprinkle the mix over the apple mix in your slow cooker

6. Cover and cook on high for 2 hours

7. Leave to cool for 40 minutes and serve

# Day Five

*Breakfast: Banana & Salted Caramel Roll*
*Time: 2 hours 10 minutes / Serving 8*
*Net Carbs: 78g / 2.75oz (26%) Fat: 12g / 0.42oz (19%)*
*Protein: 5g / 0.17oz Kcal: 440*

## Ingredients:

- 115g / 4oz cubed cream cheese

- 1 cup salted caramel sauce

- ¼ cup milk

- 1 can / 495g iced cinnamon rolls

- 4 medium bananas, cut into ¼"
  slices

## Instructions:

1. Spray oval slow cooker with cooking spray

2. Microwave the cream cheese with ¾ cup of caramel sauce and milk for 1 ½ minutes

3. Separate dough so you have 5 rolls then cut each roll into 8 pieces then add to the cheese mix

4. Pour into slow cooker

5. Cover with kitchen towel then add the slow cooker lid (the paper prevents condensation dripping on the rolls

6. Cook for 2 hours on low

7. Let stand to cool

8. Add the icing and ¼ cup of caramel sauce and microwave until warm and stir to fully combine

9. Top the rolls with the sliced bananas and top with your caramel icing

*Lunch: Cheesy Potato Soup (See page 42)*
*Dinner: Root Beer Chicken (See page 60)*

# Day Six

*Breakfast: Hot Chocolate Oatmeal (See page 28)*
*Lunch: Honey & Garlic Slow Chicken*
*Time: 5 hours 15 minutes / Serving 5*
*Net Carbs: 58g / 2.04oz (19%) Fat: 15g / 0.53oz (23%)*
*Protein: 45g / 1.59oz Kcal: 550*

## Ingredients:

- ½ cup / 16oz chicken broth
- ¼ cup honey + 1 tsp honey
- 5 finely chopped bulbs of garlic
- 1 tsp salt & ½ tsp pepper
- 700g / 1 ½ lb red potatoes, halved
- 1 small onion in wedges
- 8 boneless skinless chicken thighs
- 2 tbsp cold water
- 2 tbsp corn starch
- 2 tbsp butter
- 2 tsp soy sauce

## Instructions:

1. Toss the seasoning and chicken until evenly coated

2. Spray your slow cooker with cooking spray of your choice

3. Add the broth, ¼ cup of honey, garlic, salt, and pepper

4. Add the potatoes and onions to your slow cooker then arrange the chicken on top of the potatoes

5. Cover and cook for 5 hours on a low heat

6. Remove the chicken and cover to keep warm

7. Strain the cooking juices then return them to the slow cooker

8. Beat the corn starch and water into paste

9. Cook on high until thickened

10. Beat the honey, butter and soy sauce then coat chicken serve and enjoy

### *Dinner: Taco Ground Beef (See page 63)*

# Day Seven

*Breakfast: Brunch Eggs (See page 29)*

*Lunch: Creamy Tuscan Chicken (See page 53)*

*Dinner: Easy Lasagne*

*Time: 4 ½ hours / Serving 8*

*Net Carbs: 85g / 3oz (28%) Fat: 23g / 0.81oz (35%)*

*Protein: 42g / 1.48oz Kcal: 340*

## Ingredients:

- 450g / 1lb ground lean beef
- 800g / 28oz tomato pasta sauce
- 230g / 8oz tomato sauce (no added salt)
- 255g / 9oz lasagne noodles (no boil)
- 450g / 16oz jar Alfredo pasta sauce
- 340g / 12oz mozzarella cheese (shredded)
- ¼ cup Parmesan cheese (grated)

## Instructions:

1. Brown your beef over a high heat until cooked thoroughly

2. Spray your slow cooker with your desired cooking spray

3. Spread ¾ cup of the pasta tomato sauce in the bottom of the slow cooker

4. Stir the rest of the tomato sauce and other tomato sauce into the cooked beef

5. Layer three of the lasagne noodles over the sauce in the slow cooker, if necessary, break up the noodles

6. Top with a third of the pasta sauce evenly

7. Top with a cup of the mozzarella cheese

8. Top with one third of the beef mix

9. Repeat the layers above using the final two lasagne noodles as your last layer

10. Sprinkle the parmesan cheese

11. Cover and cook on low for 4 ½ hours

12. Serve in wedges and enjoy